DENVER BRONCOS

JOHN NICHOLS

Published by Creative Education
123 South Broad Street, Mankato, Minnesota 56001
Creative Education is an imprint of The Creative Company

Designed by Rita Marshall

Photos by: Allsport USA, AP/Wide World Photos, Bettmann/CORBIS,
MBR Images, SportsChrome

Library of Congress Cataloging-in-Publication Data

Nichols, John, 1966–
Denver Broncos / by John Nichols.
p. cm. — (NFL today)
Summary: Traces the history of the Denver Broncos from the team's beginnings
through 1999.
ISBN 1-58341-042-2

1. Denver Broncos (Football team)—History—Juvenile literature. [1. Denver
Broncos (Football team)—History. 2. Football—History.] I. Title. II. Series: NFL
today (Mankato, Minn.)

GV956.D37N53   2000
796.332'64'0978883—dc21   99-023746

First edition

9 8 7 6 5 4 3 2 1

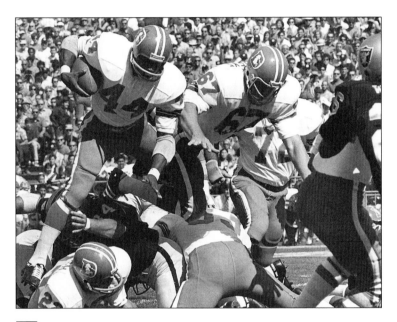

Denver, nestled in Colorado's Rocky Mountains, is one of America's most beautiful cities. Founded as a tiny cattle town before the Civil War, Denver grew rapidly in the 1870s when rich deposits of gold and silver were found in the mountains and nearby rivers. By 1959, Denver had nearly everything—stunning scenery, clean air, and a booming economy. One thing it didn't have, however, was a professional football team.

Then, in August 1959, Denver businessman Bob Howsam purchased a franchise in the newly formed American Football League. Just one year later, the Denver Broncos made

Denver's first 1,000-yard rusher, halfback Floyd Little.

football history by defeating the Boston Patriots 13–10 in the first AFL regular-season game.

The Broncos played their home games in 1960 at Bears Stadium, a 35,000-seat facility built for baseball. The team had trouble filling even that small arena in its first season, but the Broncos' popularity soon began to soar. Over the next 15 years, new decks of seats were added to Bears Stadium (renamed Denver Mile High Stadium in 1968) until it could accommodate nearly 80,000 football-mad fans.

Those fans have cheered for some remarkable athletes over the years—offensive stars such as John Elway, Terrell Davis, Floyd Little, Sammy Winder, Otis Armstrong, Lionel Taylor, and Riley Odoms; and defensive standouts such as Tom Jackson, Louis Wright, Rulon Jones, Karl Mecklenburg, Randy Gradishar, and Steve Atwater. These names have made the Broncos a powerhouse for more than two decades and have brought six American Football Conference championships and two Super Bowl titles to Denver.

1 9 6 0

The Denver Broncos opened their history with wins at Boston and Buffalo.

AN UGLY START

The Broncos have been successful both on the field and at the ticket office in recent years, but the picture in Denver was not always so bright. In fact, things were downright ugly at first—particularly the team's original uniforms.

General manager Dean Griffing, operating on a tight budget, had bought a set of horrible brown jerseys and gold pants from the sponsors of the Copper Bowl, a college football bowl game that had gone bankrupt. Completing these homely uniforms were stockings with vertical brown and

6   *Explosive defensive tackle Trevor Pryce.*

1 9 6 2

Lionel Taylor continued to spark the Broncos' offense, catching 77 passes for 908 yards.

yellow stripes. The players complained and even offered to buy their own socks, but management wouldn't listen.

The uniforms weren't the only thing ugly about the team's first year. After winning three of their first four games, the Broncos finished the 1960 season by losing seven of eight contests. Their 4–9–1 record was the worst in the AFL. The Broncos' offense revolved around passes from quarterback Frank Tripucka to end Lionel Taylor. Tripucka was a 10-year veteran of the National Football League and the Canadian Football League, while Taylor was a young player who had earlier been cut by the Chicago Bears before finding his way to Denver. Taylor would lead the AFL in pass receiving five times in the league's first six years.

After that miserable first season, Bob Howsam sold the club to a new syndicate headed by Cal Kunz and Gerry Phipps. However, the new ownership didn't do much to change the team's luck on the field. The club dropped to 3–11 in its second year, which led to the firing of coach Frank Filchock.

In 1962, new coach Jack Faulkner decided to make some major alterations, starting with those ugly uniforms. After changing the team's colors to orange and blue, he announced the "Great Sock Barbecue." Faulkner invited players and fans to a giant bonfire at the Broncos' practice field. The players, holding the hated socks above their heads, ran laps around the field. Then, to the cheers and howls of the fans, the players tossed their old socks into the flames. The new Denver Broncos had been born.

Spurred on by the Great Sock Barbecue, the Broncos stormed out to a 7–2 start in 1962. Then reality struck late in the year. The team lost its last five games to finish the season 7–7. Nevertheless, Faulkner was named AFL Coach of the Year, and attendance at home games rose more than 100 percent from the previous season.

While hopes were high in Denver, the team moved to new lows. It lost lots of games and money over the next few years. Then, before the 1965 season, Denver almost lost its team as well. Some of the ownership partners wanted to sell the club to a group in Atlanta. However, Gerry and Allan Phipps decided to buy out the other partners and keep the team in Colorado. The brothers made a direct appeal to the people of Denver. "Come out and support this team," they said. "After all, it's your own."

The fans responded enthusiastically. Season ticket sales jumped to an all-time high. Suddenly, a new tradition was born in Denver—sold-out football games. That tradition has continued: every Broncos game at Mile High Stadium since 1970 has been a sellout.

1 9 6 5

Rumbling fullback Cookie Gilchrist set a new team single-season record with 954 rushing yards.

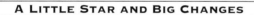

A LITTLE STAR AND BIG CHANGES

With the Broncos securely settled in Denver, the club's owners had two key goals for the future: to bring in a flamboyant new coach and to find a star player to excite the crowds. The new coach they decided upon was Lou Saban, who had previously led the Buffalo Bills to two AFL crowns. Saban was noted as an offensive genius and a master at developing the skills of his running backs. In Denver, he set his sights on a running back from Syracuse University named Floyd Little.

Simon Fletcher, the greatest pass rusher in Broncos history.

Safety Steve Atwater (#27) was known as a ferocious hitter. 11

*Speedy Floyd Little
returned kickoffs
an average of more
than 28 yards.*

At Syracuse, the 5-foot-10 and 195-pound Little had been a three-time All-American. Saban made him the Broncos' number one pick in the 1967 college draft. The coach then built his offense around Little, who used his outstanding speed and great strength to double as a running back and kick returner. By 1969, Little was setting AFL records. In one game early that season, he rushed for 166 yards, the best single-game total in AFL history.

In 1971, Little took another giant step, leading all NFL runners (the two leagues had merged into one in 1970) with 1,133 yards and becoming the first Broncos rusher to break the 1,000-yard barrier. By the time he retired in 1975, Floyd Little had established team records for most career yards rushing (6,323) and most career touchdowns (54). In his honor, the Broncos retired his number 44 jersey.

Despite Little's heroics and the strong fan support, the Broncos ended the 1971 season with their ninth straight losing record. It was time to try something different.

The changes in Denver actually started during the 1971 campaign. A trade with the New York Jets brought stellar placekicker Jim Turner to the Broncos. The Broncos' defense also got a big boost in 1971 with the arrival of colorful giant Lyle Alzado, a defensive end drafted out of tiny Yankton College in South Dakota. Alzado was as tough as nails on the field and gentle away from it. During the season, he terrorized quarterbacks; in the off-season, he made flower arrangements in the shop he ran with his mother.

Joining Turner and Alzado in Denver at the start of the 1972 season was new coach John Ralston, who had just led Stanford University to two straight Rose Bowl victories to start the decade. Ralston quickly brought in veteran quarter-back Charley Johnson from Houston to run the offense and traded with Buffalo for wide receiver Haven Moses. In their first season together in Denver, Johnson connected with Moses for six touchdowns. Rookie tight end Riley Odoms, the team's top draft pick, also quickly established himself as a fine blocker and pass catcher.

The Broncos were further strengthened in 1973 with the drafting of halfback Otis Armstrong, who had set Big Ten Conference rushing records at Purdue University, and with the arrival of defensive linemen Barney Chavous and Paul Smith and linebacker Tom Jackson. That year, Denver was not only on the verge of recording its first winning season, but also of claiming the AFC Western Division title for the

1 9 7 4

Halfback John Keyworth fought through defenses for 10 rushing touchdowns.

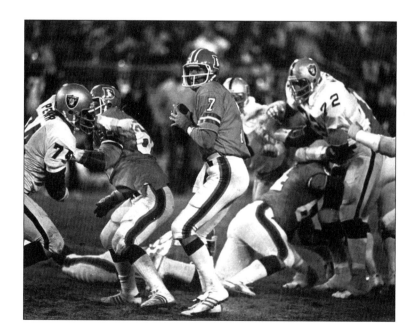

Craig Morton led Denver during the "Broncomania" years.

13

first time. Unfortunately for Denver fans, a heartbreaking 14–10 loss to Oakland in the season's final game sent the Broncos home instead of to the playoffs.

Over the next few years, Ralston continued to improve the Broncos. He made linebacker Randy Gradishar and defensive back Louis Wright number one draft picks in 1974 and 1975. The duo would serve as the backbone of the Broncos' defense for more than a decade. Ralston also opened up the Broncos' ground attack, and Otis Armstrong responded with more than 1,000 yards rushing in both 1974 and 1976. It was no coincidence that Denver posted winning records both years.

Ralston brought the Broncos to the brink of greatness, but he was not around to enjoy the results. After being criticized by team management when the Broncos barely missed the playoffs in 1976, Ralston resigned and was replaced by Robert "Red" Miller.

1 9 7 7

Otis Armstrong powered Denver's rushing attack for the third time in four seasons.

"BRONCOMANIA" AND THE ORANGE CRUSH

Red Miller ushered in a new era that sports reporters called "Broncomania" because of the wild enthusiasm that filled Mile High Stadium for each Broncos home game. Miller sounded the charge when he told reporters and fans before the 1977 season, "The Broncos will make Denver proud. We're not scared of anyone. We can beat any team."

The Denver players backed up Miller's promise, going 12–2 in 1977 to capture the team's first AFC Western Division crown. The offense, led by quarterback Craig Morton, a Super Bowl veteran with the Dallas Cowboys, made few

Outstanding cornerback Louis Wright.

Linebacker Tom Jackson was Denver's on-field leader.

errors and scored just enough points to win. The Denver defense, on the other hand, was devastating. Known as the "Orange Crush," the defense often destroyed opponents. Only one team all year scored more than 20 points against the Crush. Denver fans loved their team's hard-nosed style of play, and they packed the stands each week, dressed all in orange and waving orange banners wildly.

All of this fan support grew even stronger when the Broncos beat Pittsburgh 34–21 to reach the AFC championship game on New Year's Day against the defending Super Bowl champs, the powerful Oakland Raiders.

Played in bitterly cold Mile High Stadium, the game turned out to be a defensive struggle. The Raiders managed only a single field goal in the first half, while Denver countered with a 74-yard touchdown pass from Morton to Haven Moses to lead 7–3 at halftime.

In the third quarter, nerves grew tense as the Broncos drove down to the Oakland two-yard line. Morton then handed off to running back Rob Lytle, who tried to leap into the end zone. Lytle was met in mid-air by Raiders safety Jack Tatum, whose bone-rattling hit jarred the ball loose.

The referees didn't see the fumble, however, and ruled that the ball still belonged to Denver. On the next play, halfback Jon Keyworth carried the ball across the goal line to give the Broncos a 14–3 lead. Denver went on to win the game 20–17, earning the right to meet Dallas in Super Bowl XII.

Denver's inexperience finally showed in the Super Bowl. Dallas jumped out to a quick 10–0 lead and then coasted to a 27–10 victory. The loss was a bitter pill for Craig Morton,

1 9 8 0

Rookie defensive end Rulon Jones led the Denver defense with 11.5 quarterback sacks.

Fearsome linebacker Karl Mecklenburg (pages 18-19).

17

Kicker Rich Karlis emerged from a 478-player free agent camp to earn a starting role.

who had looked forward to beating his former team. Instead, Morton had a miserable evening, completing only four passes and throwing four interceptions.

Miller, Morton, and the Orange Crush led the Broncos back into the playoffs in both 1978 and 1979. Although they failed to win the AFC championship either year, the Broncos cemented their reputation as one of the league's most combative and successful teams. The groundwork was being laid for even greater years in the 1980s.

DAN REEVES'S BRONCOS STAMPEDE

After an 8–8 season in 1980, coach Red Miller was replaced by Dan Reeves, the NFL's youngest head coach at the time. Reeves had played halfback for the Dallas Cowboys from 1965 to 1972 and served as the Cowboys' offensive coordinator during the 1970s. All told, he played or coached with Dallas in four Super Bowls.

In Denver, Reeves inherited an aging, injury-riddled team. Reeves strengthened the Broncos' running game by drafting Sammy Winder out of Southern Mississippi in 1982. Winder quickly developed into an offensive threat as both a runner and pass receiver. Today, he ranks third behind Floyd Little and Terrell Davis on Denver's list of all-time leading rushers and touchdown scorers.

Reeves also took steps to strengthen his defense. Since many members of the Orange Crush were nearing the end of their careers, he began inserting new defensive stars— such as lineman Rulon Jones, linebackers Karl Mecklenburg and Simon Fletcher, and defensive backs Dennis Smith and

Mike Harden—into the Denver lineup. The newly built defense would strike fear in the hearts of opposing offenses for many years.

But what Coach Reeves wanted most was to build a potent passing attack. To do that, he brought in a Stanford quarterback named John Elway in 1983. The three-time All-American had earned national attention with his cannon arm and knack for making big plays.

At the start of his professional career, Elway did not want to play for the Baltimore Colts, the club that selected him with the first pick in the 1983 NFL draft. When Baltimore refused to trade him, Elway—a two-sport athlete—announced that he planned to play instead for the New York Yankees baseball team, which had also drafted him.

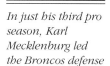

In just his third pro season, Karl Mecklenburg led the Broncos defense with 13 sacks.

The greatest punt returner in Broncos history, Rick Upchurch.

21

One of the all-time quarterback greats, John Elway.

Elway hoped that this announcement would discourage the Colts, and he was right. Baltimore finally relented and traded his rights to the Broncos. On May 2, 1983, Elway signed a five-year, $5-million contract with Denver. As the league's highest-paid rookie, he was under immense pressure to perform right away. He suffered through some growing pains in both 1983 and 1984, though he did lead the Broncos to the playoffs both seasons.

Then, in 1985, Elway began a remarkable streak, passing for more than 3,000 yards in seven consecutive seasons. During those years, the Broncos compiled a 68–42 record and captured three AFC championships.

Vance Johnson led the team in receptions (76) and total receiving yards (1,095).

Elway had lots of help on offense during those glory years. Sammy Winder was the team's rushing leader year after year, and Reeves had also brought a trio of outstanding wide receivers—Vance Johnson, Ricky Nattiel, and Mark Jackson, known as "the Three Amigos"—to Denver to catch Elway's bullet passes.

But it was Elway's courage, talent, and leadership that made the Broncos of the 1980s one of the best NFL teams ever. Elway earned a reputation as one of the greatest "Comeback Kings" of all time. During the 10 seasons between 1983 and 1993, Elway rallied the Broncos on 31 fourth-quarter, game-winning drives.

Elway's legendary status was established during the 1986 AFC championship game against the Cleveland Browns. Trailing 20–13 late in the fourth quarter, the Broncos took over at their own two-yard line. It was up to Elway to direct a 98-yard drive to tie the game and send it into overtime. He did just that, completing one pressure-packed pass after another. Then, in overtime, Elway led one more drive to set up a Rich Karlis field goal that barely slipped through the uprights. The 23–20 victory sent the Broncos back to the Super Bowl, where they lost to the New York Giants.

The next year, Elway led the Broncos on another late-game drive to win a second consecutive AFC title over the Browns. Denver faced a new opponent—the Washington Redskins—in Super Bowl XXII, but the result was the same: a Broncos loss.

The scenario was almost the same two years later. The Broncos and Browns squared off again in 1989 for the AFC crown, and Elway and the Broncos came out on top once again, 37–21. The Broncos then fell apart in the Super Bowl, however, falling 55–10 to the San Francisco 49ers.

1 9 9 2

Versatile tight end Shannon Sharpe earned the first of many Pro Bowl appearances.

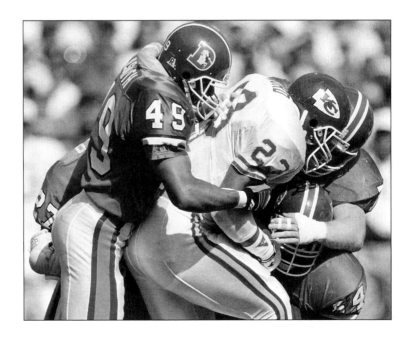

Hard-hitting safety Dennis Smith.

After Denver's embarrassing loss to the 49ers, many fans and sportswriters began to wonder if Elway and the Broncos would ever win a Super Bowl. Elway's faith, however, never wavered. In 1991, he once again led Denver to the AFC championship game, only to suffer a heartbreaking 10–7 loss to the Buffalo Bills.

Over the next three seasons, the Broncos posted only mediocre records. After a 7–9 season in 1994, Coach Reeves was dismissed, and Mike Shanahan was brought in. Shanahan had earned a reputation as a brilliant strategist during his time as an offensive coordinator in San Francisco and Denver. He had helped develop such star quarterbacks as Elway and the 49ers' Steve Young into even better players. "Mike's idea is to attack at all times," Elway noted. "He loves to put pressure on defenses by spreading them out and taking advantage of mismatches."

In 1995, Shanahan drafted a player who would prove to be a big mismatch for every defense in the league. Terrell Davis—or "T.D.," as his teammates called him—was an unheralded back out of the University of Georgia when the Broncos chose him with their sixth pick, but by the end of his rookie season, every team in the NFL knew his name. The 5-foot-11 and 210-pound runner slashed his way to 1,117 yards, giving the Broncos a deadly rushing threat.

"Terrell wasn't the featured back at Georgia, and he kind of slipped past all the scouts," Shanahan said with a smile. "Everybody thinks we were geniuses for taking him, but if we were so smart, we would have chosen him sooner."

1 9 9 5

Mike Shanahan took over as the 11th head coach in Broncos history.

The 1998 NFL Most Valuable Player, Terrell Davis (pages 26-27).

Linebacker Bill Romanowski continued to provide leadership and 100-plus tackles.

In 1996, the rejuvenated Broncos captured the AFC West title with a 13–3 record and appeared to be on their way back to the Super Bowl. In the playoffs, Denver faced the upstart Jacksonville Jaguars at Mile High Stadium. Denver was the heavy favorite, but a defensive collapse enabled the Jaguars to pull off one of the biggest upsets in recent NFL history, downing the Broncos 30–27.

Although many teams would crumble after such a heart-breaking loss, the Broncos used it for motivation. The next season, they again rode the strong legs of Terrell Davis and the mighty arm of John Elway to a 12–4 record, good enough for a spot in the playoffs as a Wild Card. Coincidentally, the first team Denver would face would be the Jaguars in Jacksonville. The Broncos destroyed Jacksonville 42–17, then won two more road games to reach the Super Bowl for the fifth time in franchise history.

This time, Denver's opponent would be the defending world champion Green Bay Packers, and the Broncos were 13-point underdogs. The game would be a tight battle throughout, but with time winding down and the score tied 24–24, Elway had the Broncos on the march. With less than two minutes left in the game, Terrell Davis capped a 157-yard performance by surging into the end zone from one yard out, giving Denver a 31–24 lead it would not surrender. The Broncos were champions at last.

"I'm so proud and happy that we could win this for the Denver fans and for John," said Davis, who was named the Super Bowl Most Valuable Player. "John Elway has meant everything to this franchise, and it's so great to see him finally get what he deserves."

After finally capturing a Super Bowl title, many fans thought that the 38-year-old Elway would retire while standing atop the football world. After all, there was nothing left for him to prove, and his body ached from 15 years of hard hits. But Elway elected to come back in 1998, though his plan was still to go out on top.

The Broncos were nearly unstoppable in 1998, ripping off 13 straight wins to start the regular season before finishing 14–2. Terrell Davis again carried the load for the team. He slashed and bulled for 2,008 yards, becoming only the fourth back in NFL history to break the 2,000-yard barrier.

The Broncos were also brutally efficient through the air, as Rod Smith and Ed McCaffrey each posted more than 1,000 receiving yards and Pro-Bowl tight end Shannon Sharpe had nearly 800. "That is one explosive ball club," said Washington Redskins coach Norv Turner after his team absorbed a 38–16 drubbing. "They just can't be stopped."

In the playoffs, no one could stop the Broncos as they rolled to their second consecutive Super Bowl appearance. This time around, their opponent was the Atlanta Falcons, who were guided by former Broncos coach Dan Reeves. The showdown between Elway and his former coach would be a one-sided affair. Elway passed for 336 yards and earned MVP honors as Denver won 34–19.

After the season, Elway announced his retirement, bringing to an end one of the most magnificent careers in NFL history. "We won't see anybody like him again for a long time," said Shanahan. "Maybe not ever."

1 9 9 9

Defensive tackle Trevor Pryce posted a team-high 13 quarterback sacks.

Receiver Ed McCaffrey made all the tough catches.

Brian Griese continued Denver's tradition of quarterback excellence.

Former Rams safety Billy Jenkins was expected to add strength to Denver's secondary.

Even with Elway gone, the Broncos remained a major threat to become the first team to ever win three consecutive Super Bowls. Talented young quarterback Brian Griese—son of Hall of Fame Dolphins quarterback Bob Griese—assumed starting duties at quarterback. Denver also added to its already strong defense by signing Pro-Bowl cornerback Dale Carter away from division rival Kansas City.

Unfortunately, a series of bad breaks quickly derailed the defending world champs in 1999. Within the first few weeks of the season, the Broncos lost Davis and Sharpe to season-ending injuries.

With the two stars sidelined, Denver's offensive load fell to such youngsters as Griese and running back Olandis Gary. Gary, a fourth-round draft pick from Georgia, showed signs of stardom as he scampered for a team rookie-record 1,159 yards. The poised Griese, meanwhile, showed veteran savvy in the pocket and threw for 3,032 yards in his first season as a starter. Still, the Broncos struggled in close games and finished the season 6–10.

Despite the disappointments of 1999, the future appears to hold plenty of promise for the Broncos. With the return of a healthy Terrell Davis and the continued development of such young standouts as Gary, Griese, and defensive tackle Trevor Pryce, it may not be long before the Broncos are riding a "Mile High" once again.